it will never be this time again

damon ferrell marbut

BareBackPress

BareBackPress
Hamilton, Ontario, Canada
For enquiries visit www.barebackpress.com
For information contact barebackpress@gmail.com
Cover layout by Peter Jelen
Portions of this book have appeared in *Ibis Head Review*.

POEMS

This book is dedicated to
Chuc Laventure.
I can't thank you enough,
my sweet friend,
for your availability and love.

For credit, several of the first poems of this collection are influenced by ee cummings. Damon Ferrell Marbut acknowledges the use of one line from some poems of cummings, around which he built his own original work.

Now is the time, when all occasional things
close into silence, and much is brought back
like morning, all ten toes on the breakfast floor
in undead succession, a crackling
mountain chain, then gratitude prayer,
usually then you go for a smoke, the day ahead
a pending list of crimes against function,
oh body, oh your soul, yarn balls racing
past each other 'round Pluto, you'll read
soon enough they're kindred atoms dancing in light
so many dark years away.

I'm told
Paris moves with lovers, two and two
but I only see the frozen motion of memory,
a leg kicked back
between spine and Eiffel Tower,
a pair of joyless hands gripping
an umbrella beneath knuckles surprised white,
I see memory scuttle around trapped spaces
unable, then, to look forward this far
and tell itself someday coming
I'll be blue-eyed still life no longer looking back.

I stood before the lot of them
and then went solo for drinks,
later
one got laid and tenure,
one continued to smile,
one continued to smile and then died young
and one kept speaking with me
in this digital era,
a note here and there
as we aged
and encouraged one another to shine
but
sure enough when the time was right
and we'd swapped enough poems
she said
you never gracefully gave yourself death,
you're not the kind that simply
buttons his coat against the wind.

Your photograph from San Francisco, though.
My mailbox has yet to recover
from the next one of you
housed in a redwood,
smiling in pretty blue on a Wednesday.
I think of all we exchange
when we are not speaking,
I think of inertia and how
when we do not discuss love
we are frozen between two things not happening,
and so, with that,
go on now,
back to your trees,
I'll die an old man fast this way,
I promise.

I entered a mad street whose
surrounding walls angled inward
toward a deep dark mouth
into which I'd one evening walk
and call home,
I would sleep on the floor
with one half a curtain,
desperate on the rod
the curtain looking like
a Labrador's bitten ear,
perfect for a man
set to travel through chaos
one foot before the other,
each upended brick
an earthly molecule
on its last leg,
we the night as dogs
still wagging tails
at the moon.

don't close the door
on the odd heart,
don't do that,
don't live without smoke
and goodness
and ruin

This is how life must remain:
any ordinary noon,
head cloudy with loved portraits of the dead,
man hanging on to final boyhood
alone at kitchen table, sighing,
shaking in his stasis the quantum aspects of breathing,
he'll hear train whistles from young work
that dried his old hands,
the wine will be cheap and full of arsenic,
his back will hurt but hurt well and rightly
and songs through the elegant pantomime of dusk
will fill each decade of unmentioned voids
and he will stand to draw the shade, peering out.

All the fruit can rot,
the cupboard can weep,
and for sure
the whole world must burn
back down to its own beauty
and yes
the mites can dance in the mattresses
the roaches will convene
and each noise inside the castle
could be successive bricks falling
or the last heartbeat of man
but by god
do not stop this
possible
gorgeous thing of creating.

everyone knows
the minute
we're in love
we die
on a couch
alone

May I never have money
if I'm to be that self-hurried thing
in the market, scowling.
Wouldn't I
be better off envying birds
of their bread,
somewhere in the sun
grinning
?

We so do this
distant kissing
like we're moths,
fluttering,
when truly
we long for chances
to be just Sex
together
and explain
ourselves
later
over cobblestones
without life
growing in number between us.

What they say I've done
is spent too much time
saving others from the fire.

If only.

If only I could roll up
into a wheel of a man
and travel the lines
of my history
to see for myself
if this was ever so.

Do not
too quickly
open the
window when
I go.
Let me
sigh the
last line
so it,
the book
of me,
can end.

The morning
has become
this long thing
indecipherable
by its anger

we

are never
climbing
from
our mothers' wombs
in thinking this way

are we?

He holds the bar door open for her
and I smile at them in the dark
I see
the vein strain on his lovely arm
I hear
him sing Dear Prudence behind her

It is exactly 6:57 in the morning
It will never be this time again

The world waves me off
as a pause becomes memory
and
love is gone fast through the glass door
while on this side of Royal Street
the sun peeks out
and madness is working out just fine.

It's been caught now, the confusion.
I ball it up like a disposable poem
and empty my heart of (how he
would not accept my love) it
made me powerless, for a while,
and then mad.
Now that it is over
I watch the dawn come
like it's delivering something.

What I wish,
if I am allowed to wish at all,
is for the ability to sleep.
That is for myself.
As for others,
there must be smiles that cause great aching,
wine for days,
sex if necessary.
But above all else,
I wish everyone's ear
to meet a chest
and something from that is learned.

My arms, sad,
challenged by absence.
There is no longer
that familiar body between them
where they would surround the lower ribs.

How dare I forget that cages are borrowed.

I feel bone-deep the turn in my elbows
that once found home about his skin.
I am up each morning and I hear them, my arms,
reaching out in moans for what is gone.

I'm not perfect on the outside
like you, still, on your outside
but if we see one another
in a theater and I am reading
and you are watching please don't hesitate,
we can interrupt the world,
I can hold you and be held by you
a final time and then we'll go about things
the way you like us,
two hearts beating themselves stiff in the ice.

French Quarter I sigh
looking at you
through a bar door at dawn,
sun slicing gently the lower parts
of trees past beaten trash cans
on the street,
Dylan on the jukebox,
rum in others,
whiskey in me,
a few disparate raindrops like snowflakes falling
over weathered hobos barking
at their lost minds,
casually spilt blood
sometimes
I sing dwindling falsettos like a howl
toward the burnt bold bearded curves of morning
acting like it is privy
to the only sun in the cosmos,
so,
damned dank silly you,
I wish you'd climb into the backdrop of my photograph
as if you were walking through me instead
and say in a growl that it is I
that old fucking danger
whom all of the world has been teased by
but still wants to touch, over and over.

So what of the pills, doctor,
and so what of
re
cover
ing
I cannot think or walk a straight line
without clamoring for the bottle of white ones,
will they help with nausea, doctor,
am I to sleep at odd hours and forget a week
and did you warn me it would take hours
to mix salad in the kitchen,
that I'd be driven to the store
just to lose how it is I choose tea,
I am trying chamomile now
sipped from a penguin mug
and it is 2:07 in the morning,
my fingers more natural on the keys now,
doctor,
I suppose I left out that part when we spoke of what ails
and tubes protruded from me like tentacles,
I suppose I was far too dazed to whisper
"bring me closer to death so long as I can still do this."

He is briefly curious, briefly young,
shredded gum lining his mouth like chaw,
slender fingertips smoothing rough baseball stitches—
they are telling him a story,
one he must convert to action and then retell.
Coach told him "tunnel vision, son"
and he develops it, astutely, seeing with eyes closed
the story turning in leather against his heart,
movement forced from mitt to mitt.
Everyone is watching, he worries,
I am alone, I am small, the world is large.
His toe presses forward and right,
ankles heavy, everything is on them,
his body pivots, a knee finds God,
an entire human nation is folded together and extended out.
He hurls himself at life in the night.
I can barely continue, he grunts in silence,
the sweat distracts him, the crowd a mad black sky
and then he lets go, the sweet violence coming
one of two sounds, beat leather or the proclamation
of slowly damaged wood reacting to the war of speed.
Everyone wants this perfect moment, he thinks,
everyone is noise tugging me from dirt,
I am going home if this ends,
I will kick my cleats on pavement and ride quietly in the back,
Mother will sing, I will feel her arms on my shoulders,
heavy, when I sleep,
I will wake at 4:30 in the morning
twenty-seven years later,
still on the mound, breathless and frail.

you only
know your suicide
by
looking back at it,
curious

It was an old Jeep
sleeping outside a lonely house,
gifted furniture on the downstairs,
a desk to write on,
beer boxes stacked to the ceiling.
I'd been half-dead holed-up
finishing two novels at once,
new poems, too, and getting scraped up
off bar stools in Florida so I'd make work on time
a state away. Lovely youth.
One October morning
I suppose I'd lost it at some job
and gave up and took my extra money downtown
and stayed in a hotel for days and took lovers like pills,
befriended a drug peddler and made it home later
in the old white vehicle dumbly doing my bidding.
Just before Halloween the phone chimed,
a girl I once lived with and wrote with saying
I am alone and I wish you were here,
so I did some blow off a ream of blank pages
and hurled my body there in the Jeep,
high on beer and powder,
stopping only to piss and buy a cassette to drown out voices
suddenly alive on the highway.
When I got there we hugged and fell in love for the moment,
she was beautiful and I, a liar,
but I was there and she was smiling,
I met the one out queer in town and we took to his bed
and then I came back to her late in morning.
I got sober a bit that next few days,
we watched Planet Earth and ate takeout
and slept beside one another, connected,
not slashed apart by sorrow,
we clung together and let dawn teach us of leaving,
we dreamed about opening a cafe,
we knew something like what eventually happened would happen
because we'd been there before,
me on the West Coast and her in Italy,

we knew she'd go to Honduras just before the coup,
I'd disappear on the road, we'd lose touch and spiritually claw out
each other's eyes and then make it back to our pages,
older and worn, fingertips dangling over sheets or screens
or bar napkins. Both of us alone.

The last card game I was in
there were naked men and women,
a refrigerator filled with beer
and I mean beer, a fridge separate from the main one,
I wasn't even playing cards, really,
just holding them in my hands, watching the other game
of women drunk and kissing women,
sun-coming-in-window-sort-of-morning,
I kissed two straight male friends, drunk,
one took off with a lady
and sex happened in the front room,
I was the only one on LSD,
crying each time I laughed because all was beautiful
and the Earth still promising,
I'd a better body then,
everyone cheered each other on to do more, be more,
love more, experiment, lay your cards down, all,
but I was thinking how Hemingway said,
"In order to write about life first you must live it"
so I didn't let on to what I was doing,
I just watched and didn't fold.

save me
from a beating
or give me one

let me
hurt alone
to learn

Burying the dog with Papa,
I held the flashlight at night in the backyard,
couldn't tell you the temperature or about the stars,
just the sound of his shoe on shovel unearthing earth.
He'd come over for this,
perhaps Nannie was inside with coffee and Ma,
discussing how a child might learn of loss.
I was fascinated. I held the light still.
The little, old poodle had been ready to go for years.
What caught me was maybe twenty years later,
seeing Papa go. And after so many visits,
huddling close in the kitchen with him
while the women chatted across the house,
I learned community and laughter and that
the world is fine when you've got tea brewing
and chicken in the fryer.
I became a man, developed trust,
wanted to become the best southern chef alive,
didn't even mind church.
None of this to suggest I was a good boy,
but I was something else then, pure,
loved to make Papa laugh,
and when my father died and I saw him buried
all I thought was give Papa some money,
give my mother money,
and I did and I went back and forth
between certainty and guesswork and,
for some reason tonight I can hear my grandfather
saying Let Me Go, Sweetheart,
You Make Me Some Kind Of Proud.

you're falling in love
off a dock
on waterfront
in Maine
I say
please continue

I heard him say this years ago,
perhaps at the streetcar-line diner on the avenue,
maybe over a cigarette in the French Quarter
a million years ago now,
after scientists left with their findings
and wrote books on the earth layers of our talks.
The vapor of it,
the haunting remnant keeping me awake, still,
was his reminding me
(before evolution took its toll)
that as long as I live as an albatross
I'll be gliding only,
known as just a word,
and then he laughed and said,
"so on your way to nothingness
go ahead and fall down stupid in love."

I am going to be the tip
of the moistened paint brush
before it knows its color,
before sensing heartbreak
and going soundless in to the stain of itself
and left with the painful thing of longing,
to snarl out like a tsunami its story,
abandoning then some kind of aftermath
only musicians and planets
can leave behind
in the forgiveness of dust.

Is it really goodbye to the bars
and how do I replace them
how
American will it get in the dry season,
will
the whimper of torn cartilage
sing dark, more coherent tones,
and are the grimaces more pronounced
in checkout lines and train stations,
the curmudgeon in me at last paroled,
is it
a different bath now for empathy,
a more considerate rinse
of Body hiding Dance from dermis down,
my zero gravity bones in the red-black vacuum
sucking cells and building breaths to come up
less reflux and more steadied heart,
oh,
here again a changeling at half-life
and still so numb to the story of lonesome carbon,
what with wisps of old madness
curling and volleying through wind to dismantle memory
of gone, gone loves, pillars of salt, grinning,
and the hell of it all, to hell with it anyway,
it is clearer, now,
how familiar I must be when I am gone.

When I leave her
it is to do something she also does in dreams.
I run, not through her imagined meadow
or evening cul-de-sac,
nor down an old dark alley of my youth,
but with simple, unutterable motion,
a lolling tongue internally furled against my heart
kept warm against the cold life of earth
skimming surface of land,
uncoupling me then stacking me into unreadable paper,
my leftover parts the afterthought of atoms.
As she sleeps and travels
her sigh sounds like surrender more so than breath,
her tail curled toward the bathroom light
and nose pointed always at the hall.
Her meditation is of descent,
of stopping halfway down the stairs
to peer through wooden spindles at soft light born before the sun.
She sees I am returned from some experiment in neglect.
Her voice cracks falsetto then higher squeal then, anxious,
she barks. She can't seem to say enough.
I move my right leg away from the chair at the table
and she knows it is her turn. It is her turn to watch me come down.
Her hound nose scents everything, even my hair.
She wants to know what I have learned.
I cradle her ears and fold them one at a time over her eyes.
And somewhere, surely, a rooster.

If it were just morning
then they would just be mountains,
daybreak cones of earthen sky marrying themselves,
just that,
and yet, instead,
it is altogether a soft dream
as if something were dying,
as if something had to die,
a carnival of dust one hundred feet back,
then times that by eight—
farther climbing faster further up higher faster—
the wind leans in, quiet,
your joy is yours, but first, pain
then gravel air spiraling into clouds,
I say I am seeing this,
commanding it, even,
to leave if it is just leaving,
there's only sun now coming,
and forest, and river,
something else, now, too,
at the tip of my tongue.

She speaks of vertigo
with a collector's sense of ownership.
It is hers.
Something to bundle with the spells,
with an erstwhile dizziness fogging memory,
enough to send a witch to fire.
And then nausea, too. The pills may cause it.
The pills do not cause it, she says.
Perhaps ten years ago this morning,
still in bed and tucked like an otherwise sated child,
confused and sure at once,
her mind the only energy to snarl at what is true,
what cannot be true,
that what was once so morbid
had become working fact,
that machines short circuit,
something breathing will some day stop breathing,
that waking face down in the bathroom trash
is still, and mercifully, the worst that there is.
She is still speaking.
To still be speaking is hers.
I carry hundreds of pounds of mulch and topsoil
from truck to yard.
She wraps her forehead with a towel,
saying, I can take it from here.

It has been nearly two decades now
and yet
in your death and of my breathing
I drift, silently, waiting to be snagged
by the hook of how I memorize you, still,
an unturned bookless page with no home,
furled and eaten by old torrents
now so soft
I put my ear to the world to hear you smiling,
I divide myself between kept lips
and the absence of them—
I do not wish to give up on the math of you,
wanting you in nature, *still*,
every single moment
covered by the thought of rain,
then the dew of you,
clinging on in morning for the light.

She mentioned bay navel oranges
and instantly I began again to dream,
not far past morning's pull
of mountain trail shadow
and the hither whisper of streams.
No. Those were real and sealed in bunkers
warmed by nights of war.
I do not know much light for such things.
But a lambent trickle of dancing bright blood
from my fingertip to hers
and outward burst the memory
she didn't know she'd given,
the lightest version of me, a boy,
floating over water toward death and revival,
an adolescent violence uncorrupted by reason,
flight, the un-roughed upward-ness of palms, asking,
and sunlight, her hair now in wind,
I see her smile in years before I'd know her,
a girl, ever a girl, insisting.

If I seemed to be dismissive
I concede my thinking was wrong.
Who knew I'd be such a cynic on the pillow.
What if my one closed eye told the story of the other.
What if both of them lied.
I didn't mean the joke to work against you.
Maybe if you'd not gone cold in bed.
Maybe if that.
I know all the greed in the world when it comes to you.
Next time,
and I pray there is one,
you'll fold backward in to me
and I will lie awake thinking of you in that dream,
you, under water,
bubbles rising over your hair,
you, safely having found me,
saying, I will exhale and come up.

The snow, as she predicted,
turned to road ice like needle to addict.
Bread went sparse at market.
I did not stand at the window
observing the heavy sag of white water
tamp my car beside a tree picked bare by season.
In the corner of the apartment,
my body a soft geometry,
the quiet longing was instinct:
I miss the South without romance,
I am more South than this mountaintop.
It was body that took trips
and jobs and did escapes,
brought them back to heart and said,
please explain me to myself now that I am home,
every inch of it, each speck of dirt,
every whispered old drama
and the open graves of each pressed breath speaking.
Tell me all of it.

It is no more complex than air.
All those moments of, oh,
the gait of love shuffling to approach itself,
of watching you watch love move.
Sometimes aghast.
Sometimes with bright humor.

More times than not, just a cigarette flick still red
finding dark pine cones off the evening terrace—
that was at least what we could see,
everything waiting to combust.

You asked,
How are you always such a mistake.

And you rebuked me for the roadways
and the mountain cliffs,
the coming just in time to leave,
just leaving it and us like that.

Without me you bought flowers.
You sent the photograph,
a tabletop of lavender flags.
I could be wrong about the color.

You said,
Heartache speaks backwards once the pain subsides.
I asked,
May I move in to those flowers and live forever.

You told me how in the photograph
I looked like a writer who had labored in a factory.
So what was it. What did you know.
Was it the long, drawn snarl of scarring
down the outside of my forearm,
forever steeped in past bleeding,
well of course,
that has grazed you when we touch,
but did I whisper to you in bed about the chemical smell,
the taste of shaved caliper and salt,
had I ever covered the night I limped and chafed
until morning and my skin had quit and taken to sorrow
apart from me, like I at last owned simply nothing,
or perhaps I mentioned the slump-shouldered soda lines,
the men and women with their white bread bologna stacks,
warning clock above the closed deli
in the beleaguered hours past midnight and did I speak to
a spent ecstasy holding together the last subtle glow of my vision
past the forklift drivers and the machinists' downward stares,
did I speak to how I discovered forgiveness there
amidst walls of hidden acid and metal set against my bones,
I must have covered the thickness of every finger,
all the earned dirt, the increased density of mine,
tunnel-heavy like they could pierce a mountain for roadway
but losing fast how to grip a pen and tell of it,
the shrill song of waking pain before noon, the dreams of pain,
the ghost of two functioning arms, a spine that craved death,
the elbow patches of missed black sediment
ignored by a worn breakfast time bath,
did I tell you the gift of collapsing from this
in the stark perfect cruelty of the Carolinas
before this other blemished but needed thing,
when we turned on an axis in the dark of your room
and one of us kissed the other's back,
high in the middle,
where the stories continue beginning, ending.

I came up insane
and hadn't burst yet in to ether
but I knew then
how as a blur we're always beautiful
and fear cannot find us

and
you came up a mindless, spent dreamer
too soon wearing late dusk
like burial cloth heavy as the first guilt of sex,

and
I came up a mad and fatherless boy
gasping out galaxies of gravity and lust,

and
together
we came out pure and wild,
unbridled gifts of life light in morning
and for us it was my cracked-sycamore voice,
your percussive heart,
our ten small fingers signing inborn songs:
this doesn't end,
forever never ever stops.

Her flagship madness was also mine,
in a late night bar
I stood hip-snug and leaned close
to the man with the bottles, tab open,
a drunk boyhood neighbor slapping me
on the arm but I was watching as the bruise came on,
she was dance, she was dervish,
pregnant with who knows what number child,
what form of sprite or fey groundling
set to burst from her beneath the unsure aerial work
of her mother-ness,
I'd heard her sing across town
and it hurt my body to listen,
more ache than labored orgasms
or the first taste of enlightenment,
she was drug-sick, she'd omniscient eyes,
the man quit hitting me and took to a corner
to cry in his flannel and she still danced,
she spun, she upside-downed,
her shoulders leapt over her ankles,
a torn shirt caught its frayed counterpart in a whirl
against the backdrop of police lights through the window,
I was drunk and suddenly everything was soundless,
I was found in some unafraid loneliness,
she approached me as if we'd known one another
since Christ bled and I said nothing,
she touched my pained arm and whispered,
I am a warlock
and then she was gone.

About the Author:

Damon Ferrell Marbut is author of the poetry collections *Little Humans Accidents*, *Human Crutches*, and *garbageflower*. He is also author of the critically-acclaimed novel *Awake in the Mad World*. Damon lives near and works on a vineyard in the Blue Ridge Mountains of North Carolina.

Also by the Author

Awake in the Mad World

Little Human Accidents: Chaos Poems from the Brink

Human Crutches

garbageflower

BareBackPress

Also from BareBackPress

Better Than God
Peter Jelen

Euthanasia is a firing squad, the Catholic Church brings the
Son of Man back to life with the Shroud of Turin, doctors
create imaginary mental disorders to further their careers, and
God hands in his letter of resignation in the form of a suicide
note while lonely young girls seek out pedophiles on the
Internet just for some attention.

Better Than God is a collection of dark and humorous
fast-paced imaginative stories filled with unforgettable
characters only Peter Jelen can provide.

Better Than God
$12.99
6" x 9"
254 pages
ISBN-13: 978-0988075016
ISBN-10: 0988075016
BISAC: Fiction / Short Stories

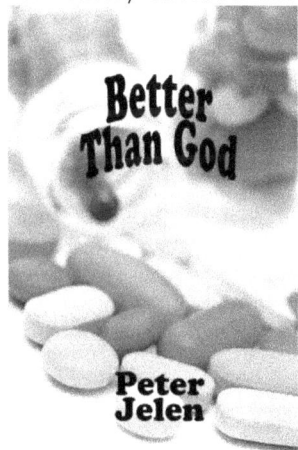

Knuckle Sandwiches
Wayne F. Burke

Knuckle Sandwiches is a punch in the face to art, culture, and society. A smack in the mouth to propriety. Knuckle sandwiches of the literal kind as well as the more common, but no less painful, metaphorical kind, which life gives to everyone regardless of race, creed, class, or gender.

Knuckle Sandwiches
$14.98
5.25" x 8"
116 pages
ISBN-13: 978-1926449081
ISBN-10: 1926449088
BISAC: Poetry / General

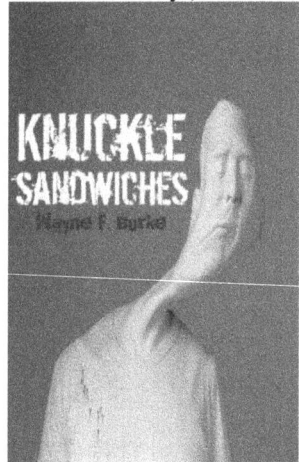

garbageflower
Damon Ferrell Marbut

With garbageflower, Damon Ferrell Marbut demonstrates once again how each book is its own unique expression of human engagement. The generosity of this collection comes from the shared moment, wherein often Marbut leaves defining the poem's purpose up to the reader. Other times there is no doubting how firmly he believes there is no line separating abstraction from reality. This believable, touching book of poems is for everyone.

garbageflower
$15.00
5.5 x 8.5
102 pages
ISBN-13: 978-1926449074
ISBN-10: 192644907X
BISAC: Poetry / General

Heaven's Gone To Hell
Andrew J. Simpson

Heaven's Gone To Hell leads the reader through a series of humorous dystopias that challenge the way we use language and the way we see the world. From alcoholic archangels, to heaven's reliance on unpaid labour, to a devil just trying to do what's right, Andrew J. Simpson's follow-up to The Big Picture turns the tropes of society on their ears.

"The mind of Andrew J. Simpson is an ideas machine … His brain is actually a powerful alien computer."

~ *Alejandro Bustos, Apartment 613*

Heaven's Gone To Hell
$19.99
6" x 9"
174 pages
ISBN-13: 978-1926449067
ISBN-10: 1926449061
BISAC: Fiction/ General

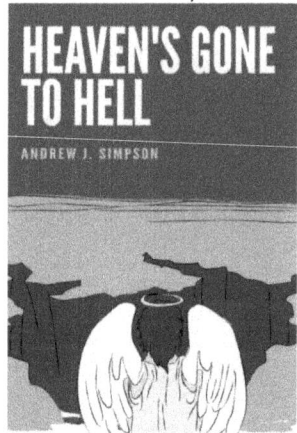

Remote Life
Edward Anki

Remote Life slices into the reader's mind like a paper cut, provoking thought, mild discomfort, and the unsettling thrill of a direct and immediate experience of reality. In this collection of poems, Edward Anki addresses the disconnectedness of modern urban existence in raw and unforgiving terms, offering an unfiltered take on everything from the struggles of dating to the stark actualities of aging and death.

Remote Life
$10.00
5.25" x 8"
46 pages
ISBN-13: 978-1926449029
ISBN-10: 1926449029
BISAC: Poetry / General

Impressions Of An Expatriate: China
Peter Jelen

Impressions Of An Expatriate is an honest, firsthand examination of one expat's experiences living in China dealing with culture shock, racism, and assimilation. From his encounters with children grown in cages to bears fighting to the death in a pit at the base of the Great Wall, Jelen's poems leave little to the imagination with haunting, vivid portraits that will take you on a trip.

"Jelen observes everything going on all around him, and as he sees it happening, he's taking it in, and becoming wise in the ways of the world..."

~ *Carl Miller Daniels*

Impressions Of An Expatriate: China
$8.50
5.25" x 8"5
60 pages
ISBN-13: 978-0992035563
ISBN-10: 0992035562
BISAC: Poetry / General

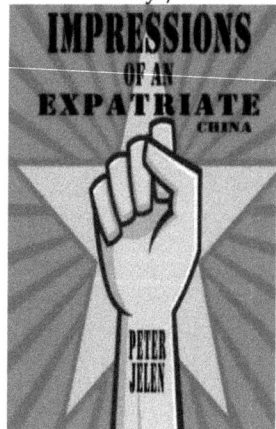

Hearing Voices
The BareBack Anthology

Since 2012 BareBack has sought to publish writers who are straightforward, sincere, and passionate. Hearing Voices: The BareBack Anthology features the most innovative and honest poetry, fiction, and flash fiction that has appeared in BareBackMagazine since its inception. Hearing Voices is bold, brave, and a great showcase of some amazingly talented new and established writers from around the world.

Hearing Voices: The BareBack Anthology
$14.99
6″ x 9″
132 pages
ISBN-13: 978-0992035549
ISBN-10: 0992035546
BISAC: Poetry / General

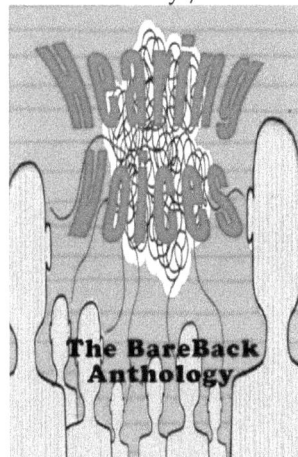

And So On...
The BareBack Anthology

A collection of innovative poetry from poets speckled around the world who have been featured in BareBack Magazine ~ an online publication dedicated to BareBack writers. People who aren't afraid to take off their gloves and give the world sincere, unpretentious, honest writing that has punch. *And So On...* is dark, humorous, and sometimes downright strange.

And So On...: The BareBack Anthology
$17.99
5.25" x 8"
134 pages
ISBN-13: 978-192-644-910-4
ISBN-10: 192-644-910-X
BISAC: Poetry / General

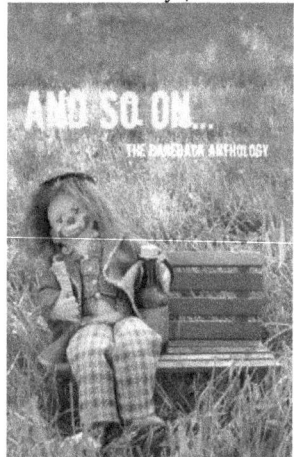

Be Kind to Strangers
Carl Miller Daniels

A wild and wondrous group of poems, BE KIND TO
STRANGERS is the most recent collection of work by Carl
Miller Daniels. Sweet, sexy, and alarming, with more than a
hint of gentle absurdism, these poems cross the paths from
sadness to joy, with a sense of awe and amazement that things
in this world, are like they are.

Be Kind to Strangers
$8.50
5.25" x 8"
56 pages
ISBN-13: 978-1926449043
ISBN-10: 1926449045
BISAC: Poetry / General

be kind to
strangers

carl miller daniels

DICKHEAD
Wayne F. Burke

One of the best volumes of poetry published this year or any
year, DICKHEAD is an absurdist knuckle sandwich that deals
in realism and farce in equal measures: simultaneously a
punch to the gut and massage--jasmine mixed with hemlock--a
ride through the Tunnel of Love and into the Fun House...An
eclectic stew of poetry that engages both soul and spleen, heart
as well as mind.

Dickhead
$13.00
5.25" x 8"
108 pages
ISBN-13: 978-1926449050
ISBN-10: 1926449053
BISAC: Poetry / General

Sedimentary Iguana-Land
Carl Miller Daniels

Sedimentary Iguana-Land, a new book by Carl Miller Daniels. The book consists of rants, musings, lists, poems -- and yes secret forbidden thoughts -- all of which Daniels had scrawled onto 3x5 cards over a period of many years, put into a dusty cardboard box, and kept there in that box, until he said what the heck, and decided to dig them out. Sedimentary Iguana-Land ~ ya ain't seen nothin' like it.

Sedimentary Iguana-Land
$8.50
5.25" x 8"
114 pages
ISBN-13: 978-1926449128
ISBN-10: 1926449126
BISAC: Poetry / General

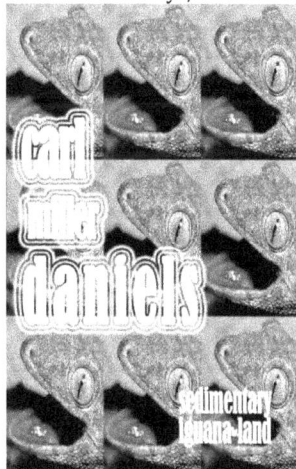

The Human Condition Is A Terminal Illness
Matthew J. Hall

To be human is to come to terms with a repetitive and trying history; an acceptance of the potential beauty and the overiding toxicity of mankind. The Human Condition is a Terminal Illness, pulls individual and societal insecurities out from our collective subconscious in an effort toward analysis and question. More often than not, in the midst of a confused, selfish, self-hating populace, the answers are left wanting.

The Human Condition Is A Terminal Illness

$12.50

5.25" x 8"

140 pages

ISBN-13: 978-1926449111

ISBN-10: 1926449118

BISAC: Poetry / General

BareBackPress

www.barebackpress.com
Hamilton, Canada

www.ingramcontent.com/pod-product-compliance
Lightning Source LLC
Chambersburg PA
CBHW050949030426
42339CB00007B/346